CRAFTS
for kids

Fancy Dress

Tessa Brown

WAYLAND

This edition published in 2007 by Wayland

© 2003, 2007 The Brown Reference Group plc.

Wayland
338 Euston Road
London NW1 3BH

Wayland Australia
Hachette Children's Books
Level 17/207 Kent Street
Sydney, NSW 2000

For The Brown Reference Group plc.
Craftperson: Greta Speechley
Project Editor: Jane Scarsbrook
Designer: Joan Curtis
Photography: Martin Norris
Design Manager: Lynne Ross
Managing Editor: Bridget Giles
Editorial Director: Lindsey Lowe

British Library Cataloguing in Publication Data

Brown, Tessa, 1963-
    Fancy Dress. - (Crafts for kids)
    1. Children's costumes - Juvenile literature 2. Handicraft
    - Juvenile literature
    I. Title
    646.4'78

ISBN-13: 9780750251570

ISBN: 978-0-7502-5157-0

Printed and bound in Thailand

Wayland is a division of Hachette Children's Books

Contents

Introduction 4

Cowgirl chaps 6

Gold watch 8

American football helmet 10

Treasure chest 12

Spring bonnet 14

Sheriff's star 16

Sweet-wrapper crown 18

Funky phones 20

Bubble wrap wings 22

Flower garlands 24

Pirate's parrot 26

Bouncy antennae 28

Patterns 30

Index 32

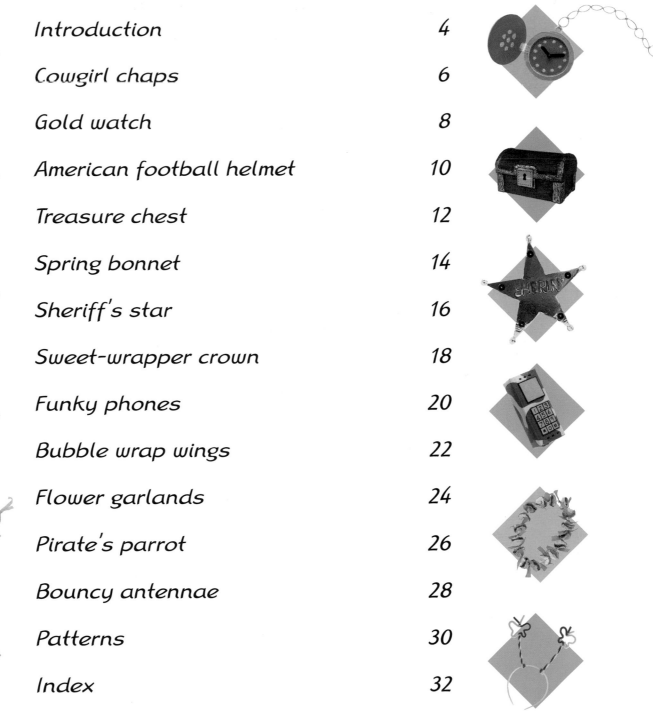

Introduction

If you're dressing up for a play or a party, take a look in this book for some inspiring costume ideas. There are pretty pastel wings for a butterfly, bird or fairy on page 22 and a parrot that perches on your shoulder on page 26. Use your imagination to adapt the projects to suit your character.

YOU WILL NEED

Each project includes a list of all the things you need. Before you go out and buy lots of new materials, have a look at home to see what you could use instead. For example, you can cut any card shapes out of old boxes. Save up foil sweet wrappers to make the crown on page 18. You can buy pipe cleaners, crêpe paper, craft foam and foam board from a craft shop. You can buy cable for the American football helmet and fabrics, such as mock leather and muslin, from a department store.

Getting started

Read the steps for the project first.

Gather together all the items you need.

Cover your work surface with newspaper.

Wear an apron, or change into old clothes.

A message for adults

All the projects in *Fancy Dress* have been designed for children to make, but occasionally they will need you to help. Some of the projects do require the use of sharp items, such as needles and scissors. Please read through the instructions before your child starts work.

Making patterns

Follow these steps to make the patterns on pages 30 and 31. Using a pencil, trace the pattern on to tracing paper. To cut the pattern out of card, turn the tracing over, and lay it on to the cardboard. Rub firmly over the pattern with a pencil. The shape will appear on the card. Cut it out. To use a half pattern, trace the shape once, then flip over the tracing paper and trace again to complete the whole shape. Or follow the instructions for the project.

When you have finished

Wash paintbrushes and put everything away.

Put pens, pencils, paints and glue in an old box or ice cream container.

Keep scissors and other sharp items in a safe place.

Stick needles and pins into a pincushion or a piece of scrap cloth.

BE SAFE

Look out for the safety boxes. They will appear whenever you need to ask an adult for help.

Ask an adult to help you use sharp scissors.

Cowgirl chaps

Cowgirls and boys wear leather chaps to protect their jeans when they're on horseback. You can make chaps of your own from mock leather or any spare tough fabric.

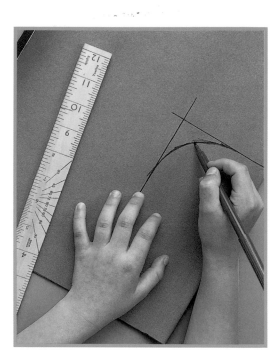

YOU WILL NEED

| two pieces of brown mock leather, each 68 cm × 55 cm (27 in × 22 in) scissors | felt-tip pen hole punch large needle red ribbon or twine ruler |

1 To make one leg of the chaps, fold a piece of fabric in half lengthwise with the right side of the fabric facing inwards. Draw a rectangle 23 cm × 10 cm (9 in × 4 in) in one corner on the fold. Draw a curved corner as shown.

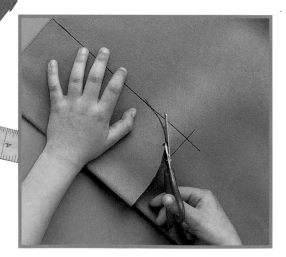

2 Cut out this rectangle, following the curved corner line. That is where the chaps will curve around your inside leg.

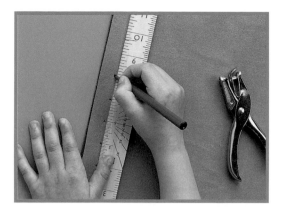

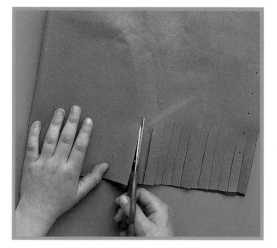

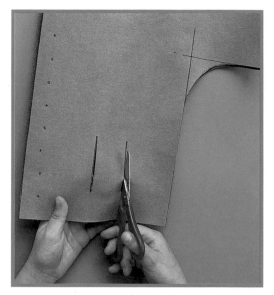

3 Make marks every 2.5 cm (1 in) along the opposite edge, about 1 cm (½ in) in from the edge of the fabric. If you are using mock leather fabric, use a hole punch to make holes where you have made marks. If you are using a softer fabric, you can use these marks as a guide for sewing.

4 Cut a fringe along the bottom edge of the fabric.

5 At the top of the leg cut two slits to make belt loops. Cut the slits slightly longer than the width of your belt. Now unfold the fabric, and re-fold it with the right side facing outwards.

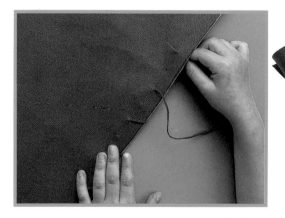

6 Thread red ribbon or string on to a large needle. Sew up the side of the leg, passing the needle through alternate holes. When you reach the top, sew back down through the empty holes to make a cross pattern. Tie the ribbon in place. Follow the steps again to make the second chaps leg. Wear them over trousers and keep them up with a belt.

Gold watch

This old-fashioned watch slips inside the pocket of a suit vest or the inner pocket of a smart jacket. It is the perfect prop for dressing up as an old-fashioned gentleman.

YOU WILL NEED

thick white foam board	black plastic container to make the watch hands
compass and pencil	
gold paint	clear plastic container to make the hinge
purple paint	
paintbrush	
gold glitter pen	thick gold thread
clear glue	
brass eye	
black map pin	

Ask an adult to cut the foam board with a craft knife to get a smooth edge.

1 Draw three circles the same size on to white foam board using a compass. Our circles each have a radius of 4 cm (1½ in).

2 Inside one circle draw a slightly smaller circle to make a ring. Ask an adult to cut out the ring and two circles using a craft knife. Glue the ring on top of one circle.

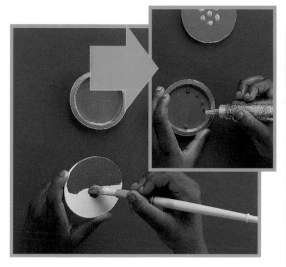

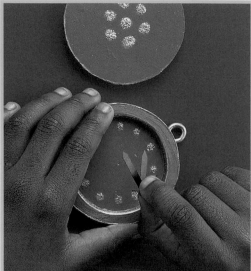

3 The circle with the ring is the watch face. Paint the back, the sides and the ring gold. Paint one side and the edges of the other circle gold, too. That is the watch cover.

4 Paint the face of the watch purple and the inside cover purple, too. Let the paint dry. Decorate the cover on either side with a pattern of gold glitter dots. Use the glitter pen to dot the 12 points of the watch face. Start with dots at 12 o'clock, 3 o'clock, 6 o'clock, and 9 o'clock, and then fill in two dots between them.

5 Screw a brass eye into the top of the watch back. Cut two clock hands out of black plastic and attach them to the watch face using a map pin.

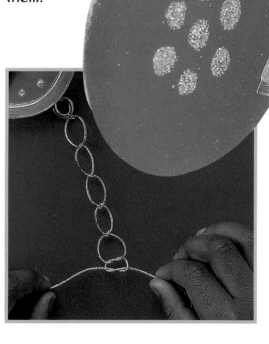

6 To make a hinge, cut a small rectangle out of clear plastic. Fold it in half and glue it to the rim of the watch face. Let the glue dry and then glue the free end to the watch lid. Let the glue dry again.

7 To make the chain, thread a length of gold string through the brass eye. Tie the two ends of thread together in knots with gaps between the knots.

American football helmet

Dress up as an American footballer with this sturdy papier-mâché helmet. Make shoulder pads from cardboard to fit under your T-shirt. You could paint stripes on your cheeks like an American football player, too.

1 Blow up a balloon and tie the neck. Place the balloon in a bowl and attach it with tape to keep it steady. Mix up half PVA glue and half water in a bowl and tear up strips of newspaper. Paste the strips all over the balloon. Let them dry. Then paste on two more layers of papier mâché in this way, letting each layer dry.

YOU WILL NEED

balloon	poster paints
newspaper	cable 50 cm
bowl	(20 in) long
masking tape	felt-tip pen
paintbrush	needle to
PVA glue	make a hole

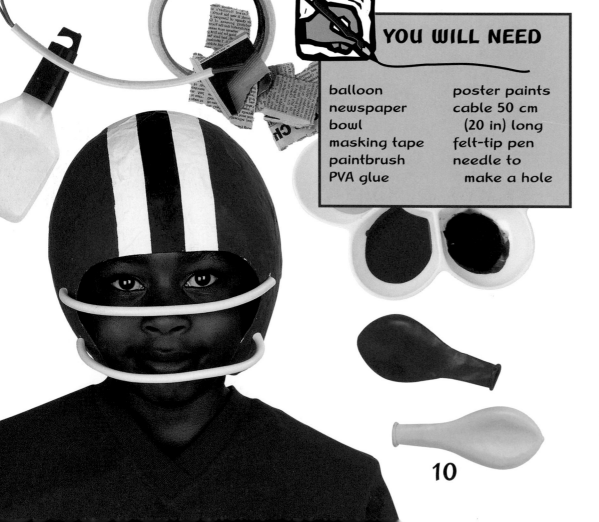

2 When the papier mâché is dry, pop the balloon. Mark on the shape of the helmet. Cut out the helmet.

10

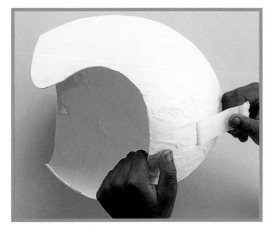

 3 Paint the helmet all over with white paint. Let the paint dry.

4 To make a neat stripe on the helmet, stick three lengths of masking tape onto the top of the helmet. They should stretch from the middle forehead to the back of the neck. The tape should be perfectly straight, each piece close up against the next. Now remove the middle strip of tape.

5 Paint along the middle stripe using blue paint. The tape will keep the stripe neat. Paint the sides of the helmet red. Let the paint dry and then carefully remove the masking tape.

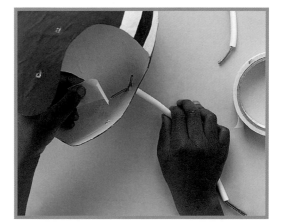

6 Make two holes on either side of the helmet using a darning needle. Ask an adult to cut two pieces of cable to fit across the helmet. He or she will need to trim the plastic coating from the ends of the cables using wire clippers. Push the wire through the holes in the helmet and attach them inside using tape.

 Ask an adult to cut the cable for you with wire clippers.

Treasure chest

This would be a great prop
to go with the parrot you can
make on page 26. Fill the
chest with gold chocolate
coins or old chains
and jewellery that
an adult can spare.

YOU WILL NEED

children's   white, brown
  shoebox   and gold
corrugated   paint
  cardboard   toilet paper
masking tape   black marker
PVA glue   pen
scissors
paintbrush

1 Cut a strip of cardboard the same length as the shoebox lid and 5 cm (2 in) wider than the lid. Glue it to either side of the lid to make a curved top. We have used masking tape to keep the top in place while the glue dries.

2 To make sides for the lid, draw around the curved sides on to cardboard. Cut out two of these shapes. Tape them to the sides with long strips of masking tape. Snip tabs along the tape so that you can fold it down easily.

12

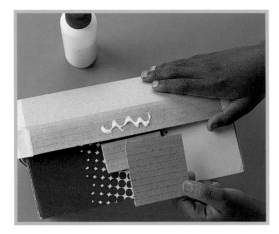

3 Fit the curved lid on to the shoebox. To make a lock, cut out two squares of corrugated cardboard. Fold one and glue it in half. Glue it to the shoebox just under the lid. Glue the other square to the lid so that it hangs over the lock.

4 Paint the box and lid with white paint. This will cover up the patterns on the box and make a base coat. Let it dry. Paint the whole box with light-brown paint.

5 To add raised edges to the chest, first mix up half PVA glue and water. Tear up bathroom tissue paper. Dip a brush into the paste and use it to push the tissue onto the chest. Build up a thick edge around the corners of the box and the lid. Let it dry.

6 Paint the raised edges with dark-brown paint. Now dry your brush slightly and sweep it across the whole chest to give the chest a realistic wood finish. Clean your brush, and then paint over the edges with a dry sweep of gold. Paint the lock gold, too, and add a keyhole with a marker pen.

Spring bonnet

Dress up as an English rose in this lovely pastel bonnet. We have used muslin, which is a light cotton fabric, but any light fabric will work well.

YOU WILL NEED

large sheet of lilac cardboard
pink muslin fabric about 1 m × 0.75 m (3½ ft × 2½ ft)
scissors
glue
pencil

gold glitter pen
double-sided tape
corrugated cardboard
large round tray
ruler

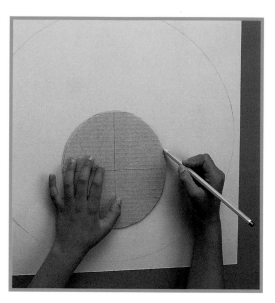

1 Draw a smooth oval about the size of your head on to scrap card. Cut it out. Now draw a large circle on to lilac card to make the brim of the bonnet. The best way to do this is to draw around a tray. Place the oval inside the brim towards the bottom, as shown. Draw around it.

2 Cut out the oval so you have a hole for your head in the bonnet.

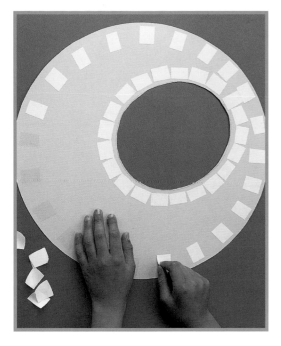

3 Cut out tabs of double-sided tape and stick them all around the bonnet on one side.

4 Place the bonnet shape lightly on top of a large piece of pink muslin, with the tape side down. Only press lightly so that the bonnet is barely stuck to the fabric. Pull up the fabric inside the hole of the bonnet to a height of about 10 cm (4 in). Now press the card firmly down on to the fabric so that it sticks in place.

5 Trim the fabric around the edge of the bonnet, leaving a border about 1 cm (½ in) wide.

6 Decorate the brim of the border with a gold glitter pen. Let it dry. Cut a wide strip of muslin to tie around the bonnet and under your chin.

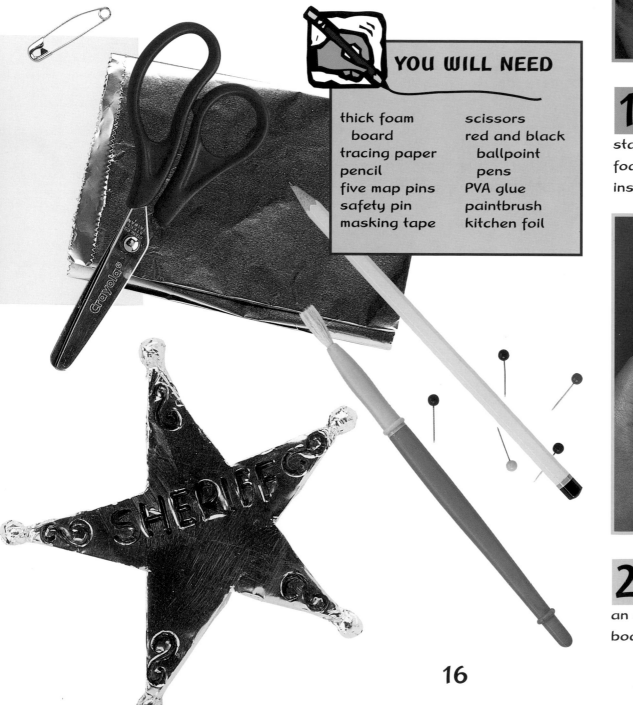

Sheriff's star

Make the chaps on page 6, tie a bandanna around your neck and add this silver badge to complete a Wild West sheriff's outfit.

YOU WILL NEED

thick foam board	scissors
tracing paper	red and black ballpoint
pencil	pens
five map pins	PVA glue
safety pin	paintbrush
masking tape	kitchen foil

1 Trace the star and lettering on page 30. Transfer the star shape only on to thick white foam board, following the instructions on page 5.

2 Cut out the badge. To get smooth edges, you could ask an adult to cut the mounting board using a craft knife.

16

3 Stick a map pin into each point of the star. Paste glue over the badge and cover it with a piece of kitchen foil. Smooth the foil with your fingers. Cut V shapes in the foil between the points of the star so you can fold it under.

4 Now put the tracing of the word "SHERIFF" on top of the badge. Go over it with a pencil, pressing firmly so that the word appears on the badge. Go over the letters with a ballpoint pen in either red or black. Add twirls to the points of the badge.

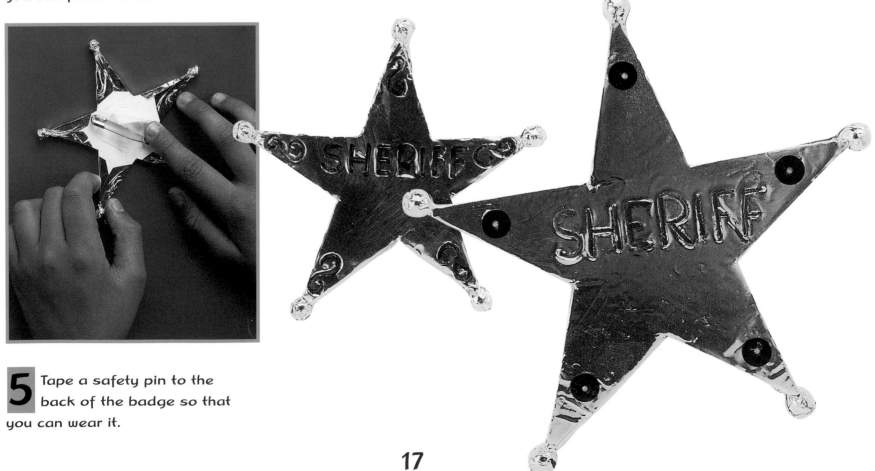

5 Tape a safety pin to the back of the badge so that you can wear it.

Sweet-wrapper crown

Make this bejewelled crown out of foil wrappers. Start saving wrappers now so you have plenty of patterns and colours to choose from.

YOU WILL NEED

foil wrappers and shiny wrapping paper	strip of cardboard 72 cm × 20 cm (29 in × 8 in)
glue	tracing paper
scissors	pencil
piece of scrap card	ruler
	acrylic paint
	paintbrush

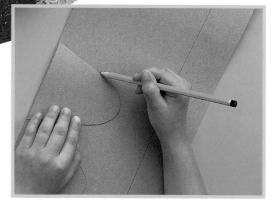

1 Take the strip of card and draw a line 5 cm (2 in) from the bottom. Now trace the rounded shape on page 30. Transfer the tracing on to scrap card by following the instructions on page 5. Cut out the shape and draw around it all the way along the top edge of the crown strip.

2 Cut out the curved shapes to make the points of the crown. Now cut off the long strip along the bottom. It will be a band to go around your crown.

3 Decorate the crown and the band with foil wrappers. Smear the card with paper glue and then press on squares of coloured foil. You do not need to cover the crown right to the bottom because the band will cover it up.

4 Turn over the decorated pieces and glue down the edges of foil to make a neat finish. Paint the inside to make the whole crown look smart. Let the paint dry.

5 Glue the band to the crown, along the bottom edge. Ask a friend to wrap the crown around your head and mark where you need to tape it so that it fits. If two points overlap, trim one down, then tape the crown together.

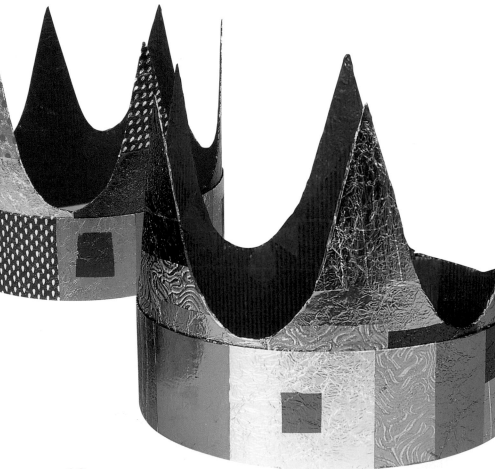

Funky phones

Bleep, bleep. Make a mobile phone for you and a friend. Dress up as city slickers for a fancy dress party and spend the whole time chattering on the phone.

YOU WILL NEED

small juice carton	masking tape
scissors	cardboard
newspaper	craft foam
acrylic paint	black marker
paintbrush	pen
	glue

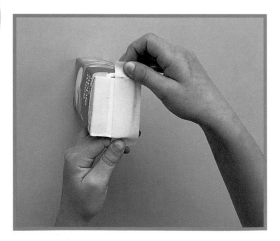

1 Cut the end off a juice carton. Wash out the carton and let it dry. Scrunch up pieces of newspaper and push them into the carton.

2 When the carton is full, tape a rectangle of cardboard over the end to keep in the newspaper.

20

3 Paint the phone with acrylic paints. Choose a few colours that are similar. For example, we have used pinks and purples. Or you could use different shades of green. We have painted on wiggles and blobs to make a camouflage pattern.

4 Cut a screen and keypad out of craft foam. Draw on the numbers, a star key, and a hash key (#). Glue them on to your phone. Let the glue dry.

5 Decorate the phone with a marker pen. Make one in different camouflage colours for your friend.

21

Bubble wrap wings

Hunt inside boxes for bubble wrap. It is used to package delicate objects so they don't break. Then you can make these wings for a bubbly butterfly. Why not make the butterfly antennae on page 28 to go with the wings.

YOU WILL NEED

bubble wrap
  1 m × 0.75 m
  (3½ ft × 2½ ft)
lime green,
  blue and
  orange
  poster paints
wide
  paintbrush
green organza
  ribbon

orange and
  green glitter
  pipe cleaners
scissors
large plate
medium-size
  plate
small bowl
black felt-tip
  pen

1 Fold the sheet of bubble wrap in half along its longest side. Use a large plate to draw curved scallops from one corner on the edge to the diagonally opposite corner on the fold.

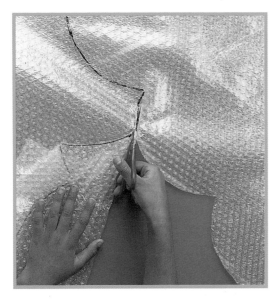

2 Cut out the wing shape along the curved lines and unfold the wings.

3 Paint the bubble side of the wings with lime-green paint. Use the widest paintbrush you can find.

4 You should have two leftover sections of bubble wrap. Paint one orange and one blue. Cut out two small circles and two medium-size circles from each coloured sheet. Use the medium-size plate and the small bowl to draw around.

5 Place the coloured circles on the wings around the edge. To attach the circles, cut pieces of glitter pipe cleaner 4 cm (1½ in) long. Bend the ends to make them into staples. Push the glitter staples into the wings around each circle. Bend down the ends at the back. Make four holes in the wings along the top edge. Thread a piece of green ribbon through each hole. Now ask an adult to hold up the wings behind your back and tie the ribbons to your arms.

Flower garlands

In Hawaii these garlands, or leis, are symbols of friendship. Make lots so you and your friends can dress up as Hawaiian boys and girls.

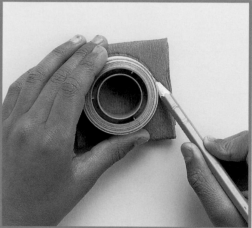

YOU WILL NEED

pale-blue, cream and green crêpe paper	scissors green felt-tip pen
pale green straws	big needle small roll of tape
string	pencil

1 Fold a piece of green crêpe paper in half and then in half again. Go on until you have a small square. Draw a circle on to the folded paper. You can use a small roll of tape to draw around.

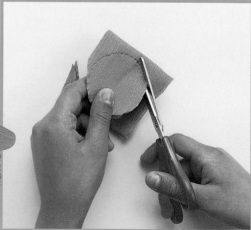

2 Cut out the circle so you have a stack of small, green crêpe circles. Do the same with the pale-blue and cream crêpe paper.

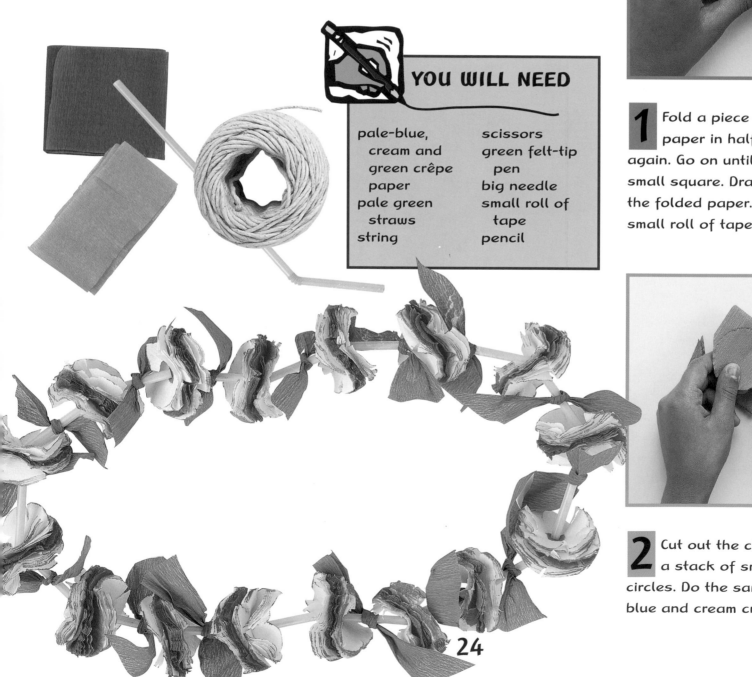

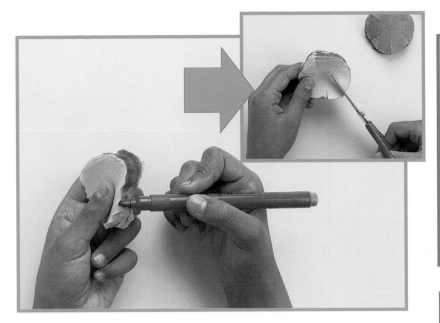

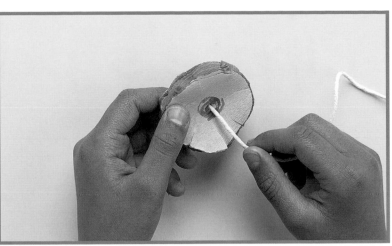

3 Use a green felt-tip pen to draw around the edge of the blue and cream circles. Make four snips around the edge to make petals. Draw on green centres, too. Make a hole in the centre of the petals using a needle.

4 To make a flower, take a few pale-blue circles, and thread string through the centre. Thread on a few green crêpe circles and then a few pale-blue circles. Cut up straws, and thread a small piece on to the string between each flower. Follow the blue flower with a cream flower.

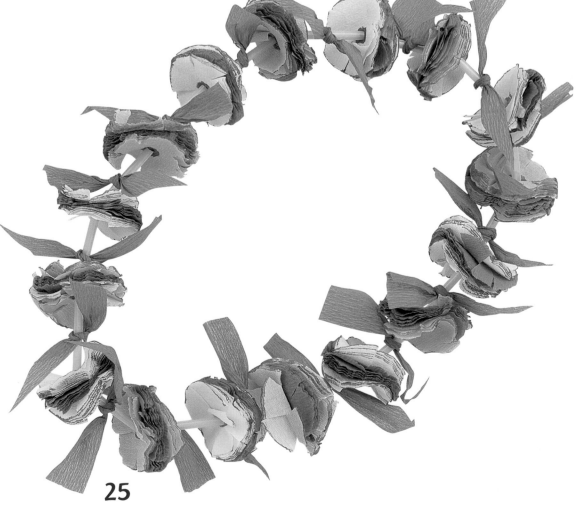

5 When you have finished the chain, tie the two ends of string together. To make leaves, cut thin strips of green crêpe paper about 30 cm (12 in) long, then cut them in half at an angle. Twist each strip in the middle and tie one around each piece of straw.

25

Pirate's parrot

Every pirate needs a pet parrot.
It is so easy to make and fits
snugly on your shoulder. Look
out for a bandanna and
an eye patch
to complete the
pirate costume.

YOU WILL NEED

corrugated
  cardboard
tracing paper
pencil
masking tape
poster paints
paintbrush

scissors
newspaper
PVA glue
black marker
  pen

1 Trace the parrot on page 31. Transfer the tracing on to corrugated cardboard following the instructions on page 5.

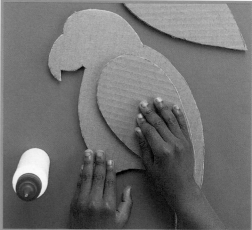

2 Cut out the parrot. Now transfer the wing shape on to a separate piece of cardboard and cut it out. Cut out a second wing. Glue the wings to either side of the parrot's body.

26

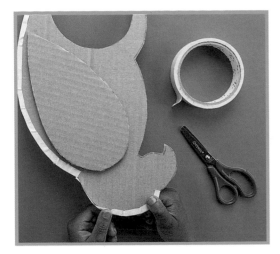

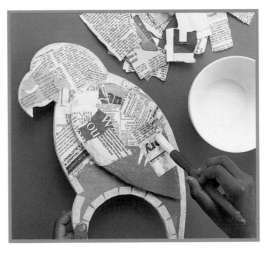

3 Make the edges smooth by sticking small lengths of masking tape all the way around the edge.

4 Mix up half PVA glue and half water in a bowl. Tear newspaper into strips and paste them all over the parrot using the watery glue. Cover the whole parrot with two or three layers of papier mâché in this way. Let it dry.

5 Paint the parrot in bright poster paints.

6 When the paint has dried, go over the features with a black marker pen.

Bouncy antennae

The butterfly antennae look cute with the butterfly wings you can make on page 22. Try making alien antennae as well, so you can dress up as a Martian or a Venusian.

YOU WILL NEED

For the butterfly antennae:	
hairband	hairband
two long, pink pipe cleaners	two long, silver pipe cleaners
two long, orange pipe cleaners	two ping-pong balls
	green poster paint
	paintbrush
	thin stick
For the alien antennae:	needle to make a hole
	glue

1 For the butterfly antennae wind an orange and a pink pipe cleaner around the hairband to one side. Twist them together about half the way along.

2 Shape the ends to make a butterfly using the guideline on page 30 and then twist them together at the very top to make tiny antennae. Do the same on the other side of the hairband to make a second butterfly.

3 To make the alien antennae, wind a silver pipe cleaner around a thin stick. Then slip the stick out to leave the spiral antennae.

4 Ask an adult to make a hole in each ping-pong ball using a darning needle. Paint the ping-pong balls green. To make it easier, push them on to a stick while you paint.

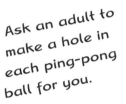

Ask an adult to make a hole in each ping-pong ball for you.

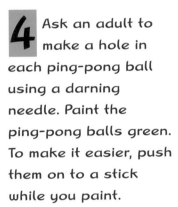

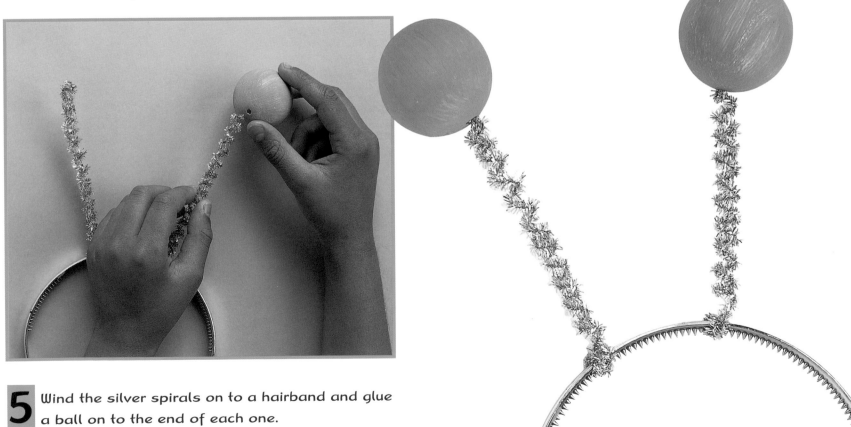

5 Wind the silver spirals on to a hairband and glue a ball on to the end of each one.

Patterns

Here are the patterns you will need to make some of the projects. To find out how to make a pattern, follow the instructions in the "Making patterns" box on page 5. For some of the patterns you need to cut out two shapes. Transfer the tracing onto scrap paper and cut out the paper template. Draw around the template to make as many shapes as you need.

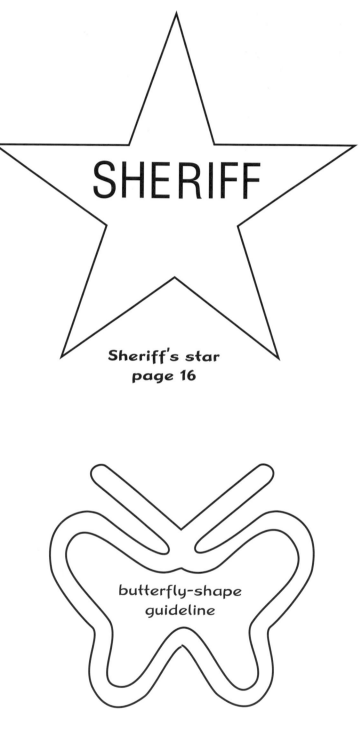

SHERIFF

**Sheriff's star
page 16**

**Sweet wrapper crown
page 18**

butterfly-shape
guideline

**Bouncy antennae
page 28**

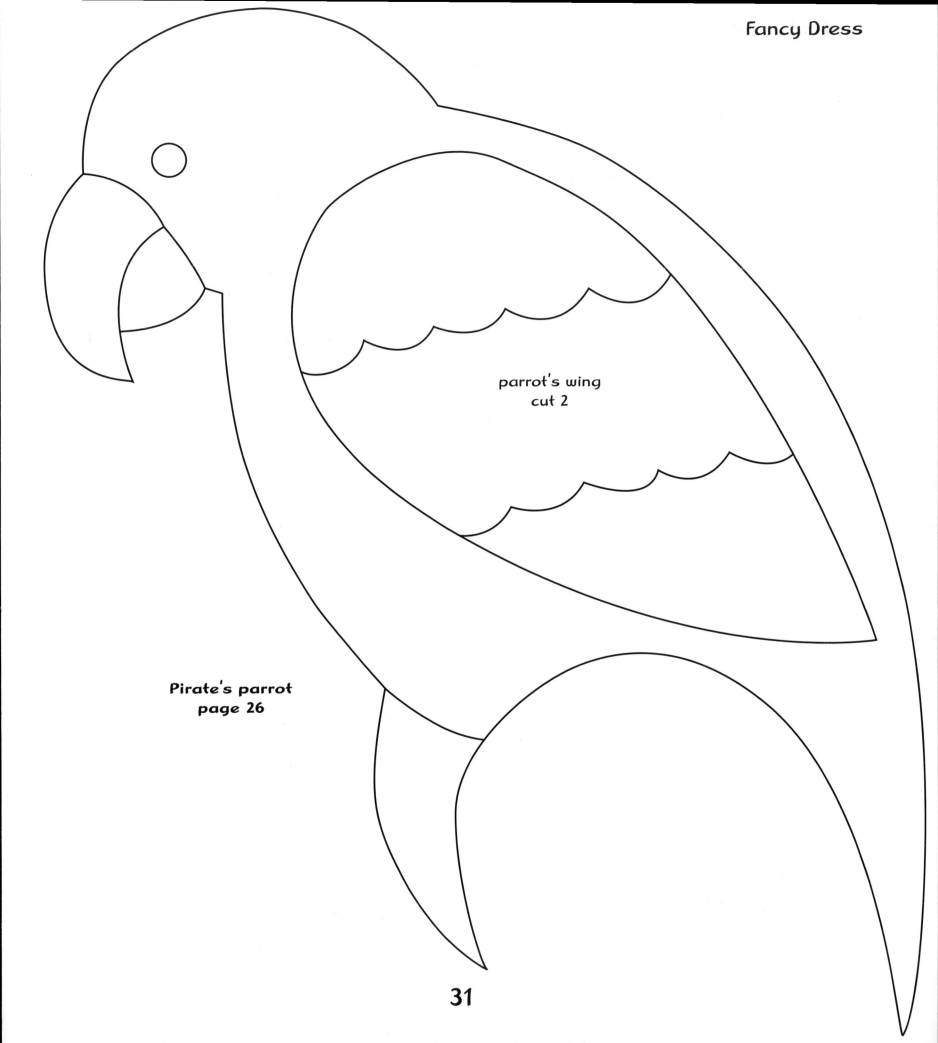

parrot's wing
cut 2

Pirate's parrot
page 26

Index

A

alien antennae
28–29

B

Bouncy antennae
28–29

Bubble wrap
wings 22–23
butterfly
antennae 28–29

C

Cowgirl chaps 6–7

F

Flower garlands
24–25
Football helmet
10–11
Funky phones
20–21

G

Gold watch 8–9

H

hats 10–11, 14–15,
18–19

M

materials 4–5

P

papier-mâché
projects 10–11,
12–13, 26–27
patterns 30–31
how to use 5
Pirate's parrot
26–27
props 8–9,
12–13,
20–21,
26–27

S

safety
guidelines 5
Sheriff's star
16–17
Spring bonnet
14–15
Sweet-wrapper
crown 18–19

T

Treasure chest
12–13